JANE *Addams*

SPIRIT
of America®

JANE *Addams*

SOCIAL REFORMER AND NOBEL PRIZE WINNER

By Pam Rosenberg

*Content Adviser: Peggy Glowacki, Assistant Director,
Jane Addams Hull-House Museum, Chicago, Illinois*

The Child's World®
The Child's World®
Chanhassen, Minnesota

JANE *Addams*

Published in the United States of America by The Child's World®
PO Box 326 • Chanhassen, MN 55317-0326 • 800-599-READ • www.childsworld.com

Acknowledgments

The Child's World®: Mary Berendes, Publishing Director

Editorial Directions, Inc.: E. Russell Primm, Editorial Director; Pam Rosenberg, Line Editor; Elizabeth K. Martin, Assistant Editor; Olivia Nellums, Editorial Assistant; Susan Hindman, Copy Editor; Susan Ashley, Halley Gatenby, Proofreaders; Jean Cotterell, Kevin Cunningham, Peter Garnham, Fact Checkers; Tim Griffin/IndexServ, Indexer; Dawn Friedman, Photo Researcher; Linda S. Koutris, Photo Selector

Photo

Cover: Bettmann/Corbis; AP/Wide World Photos: 10; Chicago Historical Society: 27; Bettmann/Corbis: 2; Corbis: 26; Hulton Archive/Getty Images: 17, 18, 21, 22; National Library of Medicine, History of Medicine Division: 14; North Wind Picture Archives: 6; Rockford College: 12; Jane Addams Collection, Swarthmore College Peace Collection: 8, 9, 13, 15, 25; Special Collections Research Center, University of Chicago Library: 19, 23 top; ; Jane Addams Hull-House Museum, University of Illinois at Chicago: 23 bottom; Jane Addams Memorial Collection/Special Collections, The University Library, University of Illinois at Chicago: 7 (neg 45), 11 (neg 22), 20 (neg 146), 24 (neg 308), 28 (neg 520).

Registration

The Child's World®, Spirit of America®, and their associated logos are the sole property and registered trademarks of The Child's World®.

Library of Congress Cataloging-in-Publication Data

Rosenberg, Pam.
 Jane Addams : social reformer and Nobel Prize winner / by Pam Rosenberg.
    p. cm.
 "Spirit of America series."
 Summary: A biography of the wealthy woman who realized her ambition to live and work among the poor and founded Hull House, one of the first social settlement houses in the United States. Includes bibliographical references and index.
  ISBN 1-59296-010-3 (library bound : alk. paper)
 1. Addams, Jane, 1860–1935—Juvenile literature. 2. Women social workers—United States—Biography—Juvenile literature. 3. Women social reformers—United States—Biography—Juvenile literature. 4. Hull House (Chicago, Ill.)—Juvenile literature. 5. Nobel Prizes—Biography—Juvenile literature. [1. Addams, Jane, 1860–1935. 2. Social workers. 3. Hull House (Chicago, Ill.) 4. Women—Biography. 5. Nobel Prizes—Biography.] I. Title.
 HV40.32.A33R67 2004
  361.92—dc21   2003006276

10 20 26

Contents

Chapter ONE

Cedarville

JANE ADDAMS LIVED AT A TIME WHEN MANY changes were taking place in the United States. The Civil War (1861–1865) began less than one year after her birth. The years after the Civil War saw a large migration of newly freed African-Americans to the North. They were searching for jobs in the rapidly **industrializing**

Chicago was one of the cities in the northern United States that rapidly industrialized in the late 1800s.

northern cities. At the same time, immigrants from other countries were flooding into the United States. They sought better lives for themselves and their families. Many of these people would also settle in the large northern cities. They found work in the factories. The men who built the factories were more than willing to take advantage of all this cheap labor. Workers were not paid much and did not demand much.

As a young woman, Jane Addams had a profound influence on many of these people. Over time, she also became an influential leader in the international peace movement. She was a woman of strong convictions who won the adoration of many and the scorn of others. At her

Jane Addams and her family lived in this house in Cedarville, Illinois.

death, though, millions of people all over the world mourned one of the great social reformers of all time.

Cedarville is a small town in Illinois, not far from the Wisconsin border. It is a little more than 100 miles (160 kilometers) from

7

the city of Chicago. John Huy Addams and Sarah Weber Addams married on July 18, 1844, and moved to Cedarville to begin their new life. John Addams purchased a sawmill and **gristmill** later that year, and the couple settled in. He went on to become one of the most successful businessmen in the county. He was elected to the Illinois senate, where he served from 1854 to 1870. His wife was also respected and well liked.

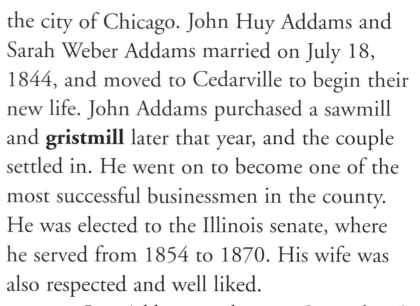

Sarah Weber Addams, Jane's mother, died when Jane was only two years old.

Jane Addams was born on September 6, 1860. She was the eighth child of John and Sarah Addams. Her family and close friends called her Jennie. By the time she was born, her family was rich. Tragedy struck, however, when Jane was only two years old. The Addams' ninth child was **stillborn,** and Sarah died just days later. It was now up to Jane's older sisters—17-year-old Mary and 13-year-old Martha— to take care of Jane, 10-year-old James Weber, and 9-year-old Alice. When Jane was six years old, her sister Martha died. Then, in 1868, John

Addams married a widow named Anna Haldeman. She had two sons, Harry, who was 18, and George, age 7. Jane and her stepmother got along well. George, who was only six months younger than Jane, became her best friend. The two were inseparable playmates who spent many hours exploring the countryside near their home.

Jane Addams as a young girl

Jane was an intelligent child who greatly admired her father. John Addams treated his daughter with respect and was happy to share ideas with her. He got up at 3 A.M. each day to read. Jane decided she would do the same. From a very early age, Jane read great works of literature such as *The Odyssey, Plutarch's Lives,* and *Pilgrim's Progress,* and she discussed them with her father. This was unusual for any child, but even more so for a girl. Jane's father, unlike many men of his time, thought that it was important for his daughters to be educated. Unlike many girls of her time, Jane was expected to get a higher education.

She wanted to attend Smith College in Massachusetts and had been accepted there. However, her father wanted her to stay closer to home and attend Rockford Female Seminary,

Interesting Fact

▶ The Addams' home in Cedarville has been designated a National Landmark. It has not been owned by a member of the Addams family since 1956.

This picture of Jane Addams was taken when she was a student at Rockford Female Seminary.

the school her older sisters had attended. Jane gave in to her father's wishes and enrolled at Rockford Seminary in 1877. She excelled in her studies there. She and a small group of friends spent many hours reading and discussing what they had read. Addams was the class **valedictorian** when she graduated in 1881. It would be several years, though, before she would discover the work she believed she was meant to do.

10

JOHN HUY ADDAMS WAS BORN ON JULY 12, 1822, in Sinking Springs, Pennsylvania. He left Pennsylvania in 1844 with his new bride and settled in Cedarville, in north-west Illinois. At the time, Illinois was just past the pioneer stage of settlement. Addams played an important role in the development of the area. He became a successful farmer and mill owner. He was the first president of the Second National Bank in nearby Freeport, Illinois. In addi-tion, he helped bring the railroad to his region. Addams spent many hours traveling to meet with landowners throughout the area. His goal was to convince them that they needed the railroad to make their farms and businesses more profitable.

Addams was active in politics and served in the Illinois state senate for seven terms. He was at the meeting in Ripon, Wisconsin, when the Republican Party was formed and was a friend of President Abraham Lincoln. The president wrote letters to John Addams in which he addressed him as "my dear double-D'd Addams."

Though he was one of the wealthiest businessmen in his town, Addams was well liked and respected by all. He was not afraid of hard work and could often be found working along with the farmhands or the hired help at the mill. He was also known for helping neighbors start businesses of their own. It is not surprising that Jane Addams grew up to have such a strong desire to help others.

Chapter TWO

Searching for a Purpose

Jane Addams attended Rockford Female Seminary, now known as Rockford College.

AFTER GRADUATING FROM ROCKFORD FEMALE Seminary, Jane Addams wanted to continue her studies at Smith College. At the time, Rockford didn't give out bachelor's degrees, so she planned to complete the necessary courses to get the degree at Smith. Unfortunately, her father still would not allow her to go to Smith. This posed a **dilemma** for her. She respected her father and wanted to be a good daughter, but she also had a great desire to be educated and work at something useful and important. Her hope was that she would discover a great purpose for her life while completing her education.

Addams returned to Cedarville in the summer of 1881. She didn't have much interest in the parties and other social events that young ladies in town were attending. She greatly disliked the domestic chores such as sewing and baking that were expected of young women. She spent much of her time reading. Then, in early August, Jane took a trip to northern Michigan with her father, stepmother, and George. John Addams became ill while in Michigan, and they decided it would be best to return home. On the way home, he got worse and was hospitalized in Green Bay, Wisconsin. On August 17, 1881, Jane's beloved father died, probably from a ruptured appendix.

Addams was heartbroken by her father's death. Even while she mourned, though, she made plans to continue her education. While at Rockford Female Seminary she had considered becoming a physician. Now she decided to go to medical school. In the fall, Addams moved to Philadelphia to attend the Women's

John Huy Addams and Anna Haldeman Addams, Jane's father and stepmother

Interesting Fact

▸ Charles Julius Guiteau, the man who shot and killed President James Garfield, was the stepbrother of Flora Guiteau, one of Jane Addams's closest childhood friends.

Jane Addams attended the Women's Medical College of Philadelphia for about six months.

Medical College of Philadelphia. Her school schedule was tough. She had classes six days a week. She worked very hard, but medical school did not excite her. Soon, she was exhausted and became more and more depressed. In March 1882, after six months of classes, Addams dropped out of medical school.

While many of her symptoms were physical, such as back pain and extreme tiredness, much of Addams's illness was probably **psychological** in nature. It was not unusual for educated young women at this time to experience the same problems she did. They were the first generation of women to receive a higher education, but many were unable to make any use of it. They were expected to return home after college, marry suitable young men, and raise families. This was the last thing that Addams wanted for herself. After more than a year of searching and self-doubt, she decided to take a long trip to Europe.

On August 22, 1883, Jane Addams, her stepmother, and several friends boarded the ocean liner *Servia* and set sail for Europe. Jane's plan was to visit 10 countries in about two years. The group traveled around Europe and visited many museums, cathedrals, and other landmarks. They went to theater and opera performances. Then, in the spring of 1885, Addams received word that her sister Mary was expecting her fifth baby and was in very bad health. She and her stepmother decided to return to the United States.

Ellen Starr was a friend of Jane Addams. The two met when they were both students at Rockford Female Seminary.

When she returned home, she stayed for a while with Mary and her family to help out. While there, she had a visit from an old college friend, Ellen Starr, and the two renewed their friendship. In the winter, Addams went to Baltimore with her stepmother. Anna Haldeman Addams wanted to spend time with George, who was there studying. When the two women returned to Cedarville in the summer, Addams found herself constantly busy running errands and helping out family members. While she was devoted to her family and happy to help out, she still longed to find a higher purpose for her life.

The first sign of what this purpose might be came while she was in Baltimore again for the winter. Bored with the social activities her stepmother loved, Addams began to do some volunteer work. She began visiting a nursing home and an orphanage and really enjoyed her time there.

Then, in December 1887, Addams went to Europe again. This time she traveled with her friend Ellen and with Sarah Anderson, a teacher from Rockford Seminary. The women toured the continent for several months. While in London, Addams visited a **settlement house** called Toynbee Hall. There, educated young men lived and used their spare time to help the poor in the neighborhood. When Addams set sail for home this time, she knew what she wanted to do with her life.

THE INDUSTRIAL REVOLUTION HAD BROUGHT WITH IT A HUGE INCREASE IN THE number of people living in poverty in London and other large cities. Many people had migrated to these large cities, hoping to work in the factories being built by the rich industrialists. Reverend Samuel Barnett and his wife, Henrietta, were assigned to the parish of St. Judes in the East End of London. They worked tirelessly to help the poverty-stricken people who filled the neighborhood.

Eventually, they decided on a **radical** new approach. They wanted to open a place where educated young men would come to live among the poor. These men were expected to teach classes and offer other services. In return, the Barnetts hoped that these future leaders would be influenced by what they learned from their work with the poor immigrants. In 1884, the settlement house called Toynbee Hall was opened in the middle of Whitechapel, one of London's poorest neighborhoods. It was named after Arnold Toynbee (left). He was a close friend of the Barnetts who died at the age of 32 after spending his life helping the poor.

17

Chapter THREE

The Project

Samuel and Henrietta Barnett founded Toynbee Hall in London, England.

AFTER MEETING WITH THE BARNETTS, Addams began to form a plan. She decided to open a settlement house in Chicago. When she told Ellen Starr about her idea, Starr was very enthusiastic. The two women formed a partnership and began making plans. Addams did not want the settlement house to just give out assistance to the poor. They both wanted to create a community in which the rich and the poor interacted on a daily basis. Addams always insisted that the settlement house was founded as much to help herself and other young women like her as to help the poor.

In January 1889, Addams arrived in

Chicago. She and Starr began calling on wealthy and powerful men and women to present their plan. Their ideas were well received by many influential people. Soon, they knew they had support to make their dream a reality. They toured the city's poorest immigrant neighborhoods, looking for a building. Addams met several times with Helen Culver, the cousin of Charles Hull. Hull was a wealthy real estate developer who had recently died. He left his fortune, including a mansion on Halsted Street, to Culver.

Interesting Fact

▸ Half of the children born in Chicago in the year 1889 died before their fifth birthdays.

The neighborhood surrounding Hull-House was home to immigrants from Italy, Greece, Russia, and Ireland. Through the years people from many other ethnic groups lived in the area. The residents of Hull-House welcomed everyone and worked to promote acceptance of people from all cultures.

Hull-House opened on September 19, 1889.

After the meetings with Addams, Culver agreed to rent a large room on the first floor of the mansion and the entire second floor for $720 a year.

Addams spent about $3,000 of her own money to fix up the building and another $1,800 on furniture. On September 19, 1889, the settlement house at 335 Halsted Street in Chicago opened its doors. Hull-House was born. Addams and Starr lived there along with housekeeper Mary Keyser. The first young woman to move in as a resident with Addams and Starr was Anna Farnsworth. Through the years, many other young women and men would spend time at Hull-House as residents or volunteers. Some of them, such as Julia Lathrop and Florence Kelley, would become well-known social reformers themselves.

The neighborhood around Hull-House was very poor. The houses that surrounded it were rickety and rundown. Each house was home to several families. The streets were not paved and often muddy. Children played near the garbage that piled up in streets and alleys. Many mothers had to work in factories, and their children were left unsupervised. Often, children also had to work in factories to help support their families. Addams dreamed of making Hull-House a place where they could experience better things.

Many adults and children enjoyed being members of the Hull-House choir.

Addams and Starr created the programs at Hull-House as they went along. A kindergarten, one of the first in Chicago, was opened on the first Monday the settlement was open. For older children, there were many classes and clubs. Some of the classes were educational, such as sewing and reading. Others were aimed at developing the children's understanding of the arts. Many children enjoyed taking part in theater productions, music lessons, and recitals at Hull-House. In the evenings, there were many classes and clubs for adults and for the children who had to work during the day. At Hull-House, they could learn to speak English, join a book club, learn about great artworks, or attend lectures on topics such as child labor.

After just a few weeks, people were flocking to Hull-House. Within two years, Hull-House was the meeting place for more than 50 clubs. Dozens of classes were held there each week. It is estimated that about 1,000 people visited Hull-House each week. It was open from 9 A.M. to 9 P.M., and Addams was always available after hours to help in emergencies. It was not unusual for her to be called out to help deliver a baby or to help comfort neighbors who had a death in the family. Through their work, the residents of Hull-House hoped to bring the poor of the neighborhood a sense of hope and a chance for a better life. By al-most all accounts, Jane Addams and her settlement house were a great success.

Poor immigrant families often lived in rundown slum houses like this one.

22

CHARLES HULL (LEFT) WAS A WEALTHY REAL estate developer. He built a mansion in 1856. At the time, his home was surrounded by countryside. Hull hoped that by moving into the area, he could attract other rich families to move west of the Chicago River. Unfortunately, that didn't happen. Instead, cheap housing went up around his mansion, and immigrants flooded into the neighborhood.

Hull moved out of his home in 1868. It was rented to several different tenants in the years that followed. The Little Sisters of the Poor, a group of Roman Catholic nuns, used the building as a home for the aged for a period of time. The former mansion was also used as a boarding house. The building was one of the few to survive the Great Chicago Fire of 1871. When Addams discovered it, much of the first floor was being rented by the Sherwood Desk Company. A family was renting the second floor.

Today, two original Hull-House buildings are owned by the University of Illinois at Chicago. These buildings house the Jane Addams Hull-House Museum and have been designated a Chicago and National Historic Landmark. The interiors have been restored, and visitors can see what Hull-House looked like in its early days.

Chapter FOUR

Advocate for Peace

AS TIME WENT ON, JANE ADDAMS BECAME involved in larger social issues. She was troubled by the high death rate in the neighborhood. She knew that it was partly because of the filth that was all around. The garbage collectors in the neighborhood were not doing their jobs. Eventually, she was appointed the first

Jane Addams worked to improve living conditions in the neighborhood surrounding Hull-House.

woman garbage inspector in the city. While she only performed the job briefly, she and those who followed her made a real difference in how well the garbage collectors did their jobs.

Addams supported **labor unions** and allowed

union organizers to use Hull-House for meetings. She was one of the original members of the Civic Federation of Chicago. As part of this group, she was a member of the committee formed to help settle the disagreement between railroad workers and factory owner George Pullman during the famous Pullman Strike of 1894. In addition, Addams and other residents of Hull-House supported laws that would improve working conditions for women and children in factories. Addams also supported the work of other Hull-House residents in the founding of the juvenile court system in Illinois.

In the early 1910s, Addams began to spend more time away from Hull-House. She had grown very close to her friend and Hull-House supporter Mary Rozet Smith. Smith had a room set aside in her mansion for Addams, and during this time Addams spent a lot of time at Smith's home. Some of her time was spent writing books and magazine articles. Her focus was now on national and world issues more than the problems of the

Mary Rozet Smith (left) was a close friend of Jane Addams.

Interesting Fact

▸ One of the first children's playground in Chicago was built by Jane Addams at Hull-House. In 1891, an art gallery was opened at the Hull-House complex that drew 3,000 visitors per week. A college extension program of the University of Chicago opened at Hull-House in the spring of 1890. People could take 12-week courses in subjects such as chemistry, history, and Latin.

Jane Addams and a group of peace delegates arrive in the Netherlands to attend a peace conference in 1915.

Hull-House neighborhood and Chicago. In 1911, she became president of the National American Woman Suffrage Association. In 1912, Addams attended the Progressive Party's convention and seconded the nomination of Theodore Roosevelt for president—a high honor, especially for a woman.

When World War I (1914–1918) started in Europe, Addams spoke out against the United States becoming involved in the war. She was elected the chairperson of the Woman's Peace Party. This was an international group of women who were opposed to war. Unfortunately, her anti-war position was not a popular one, and many people turned against her. While this was hurtful, she didn't stop her anti-war activities. In 1919, the members of the Women's International League for Peace and Freedom elected Addams president of their organization.

Addams was also criticized for her continued support of labor unions. She spoke out in defense of free speech, even for **anarchists.** This was a very unpopular opinion because labor strikes often resulted in violence. Also, many people believed that **communists** were responsible for the violence. They said that if Addams was in favor of unions and free speech for everyone, she must be a communist, too. This was not true, but it still hurt her reputation. Being less popular meant that it became more difficult to raise support and money for the causes she believed in.

By 1930, the effects of the **Great Depression** were being felt by everyone in the United States. Addams regained some of the respect she had enjoyed before the war because of her strong commitment to helping the poor. However, settlement work was not as popular as it had once been. Some people had stopped giving donations to Hull-House. Though it became more difficult, she kept Hull-House going.

In 1931, her strong commitment to world peace was finally rewarded. She received the Nobel Peace Prize.

Jane Addams's Nobel Peace Prize certificate

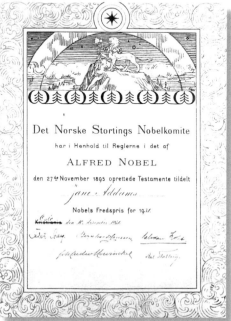

By this time, though, she was in poor health and unable to travel to Oslo, Norway, to accept her prize. Jane Addams died of cancer on May 21, 1935. During the two days that followed, thousands of mourners passed by her coffin to pay their last respects. Her funeral service was held at Hull-House, with thousands of people crowding the streets and alleys surrounding the settlement. She was buried in the cemetery in her hometown of Cedarville, next to her parents and siblings.

Jane Addams was convinced that all people, rich or poor, deserved respect. By putting her beliefs into practice at Hull-House, she touched the lives of thousands of people, not only in Chicago, but all over the world. Her willingness to speak out for world peace, even when it wasn't the popular point of view, continues to be an inspiration to those who work for peace. Though she died almost 70 years ago, her spirit lives on.

Thousands of people crowded the streets and alleys around Hull-House on the day of Jane Addams's funeral.

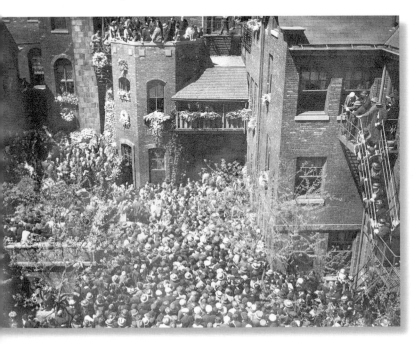

1860   Jane Addams is born on September 6 in Cedarville, Illinois.

1863   Sarah Addams, Jane's mother, dies.

1868   John H. Addams marries Anna Haldeman.

1877   Jane Addams begins her studies at Rockford Female Seminary.

1881   Addams graduates from Rockford as class valedictorian. Her father dies on August 17. Addams moves to Philadelphia and begins medical school.

1883   Addams begins a lengthy trip to Europe.

1885   Addams returns home from Europe.

1887   Addams travels to Europe again, this time for several months.

1889   Addams moves to Chicago. Hull-House opens its doors on September 19.

1894   The Pullman Strike brings national rail traffic to a halt.

1911   Addams is elected president of the National American Woman Suffrage Association.

1912   Theodore Roosevelt is nominated as the Progressive Party candidate for president of the United States. Jane Addams has the honor of seconding his nomination at the convention.

1914   Addams speaks out against the United States getting involved in World War I, which has begun in Europe.

1919   Addams elected president of the Women's International League for Peace.

1931   Addams is awarded the Nobel Peace Prize.

1935   Addams dies on May 21.

1967   Jane Addams' Hull-House Museum is opened.

anarchists (AN-ar-kists)
An anarchist is a person who rebels against the government or another group in a position of power. Jane Addams spoke out in defense of free speech, even for anarchists.

communists (KOM-yu-nists)
A communist is one who supports a system of government in which all the land, houses, and factories and their profits are distributed equally to all members of the community. Many people believed that communists were responsible for labor strike violence.

dilemma (dih-LEMM-ah)
Someone in a dilemma must make a difficult choice between two alternatives. When Jane Addams' father wouldn't allow her to go to Smith College, she was faced with the dilemma of trying to be a good daughter, yet wanting a good education.

Great Depression (GRATE de-PRESH-un)
A period in America beginning in 1929 during which there was less business and many people lost their jobs. By 1930, the effects of the Great Depression were being felt by everyone in the United States.

gristmill (GRIST-mil)
A gristmill is a building with machinery for grinding grain. John Addams purchased a sawmill and gristmill in Cedarville, Illinois.

industrializing (in-DUS-tree-uhl-ize-ing)
Industrializing refers to building up businesses, especially factories. Both immigrants and newly freed African-Americans went North in search of jobs in the rapidly industrializing cities there.

labor unions (LAY-bore YUNE-yuns)
Labor unions are groups of workers joined together to protect and further their interests. Jane Addams was criticized for her continued support of labor unions.

psychological (sy-kuh-LOJ-ih-kul)
Something that is psychological involves the mind. Jane Addams's illness after dropping out of medical school was probably psychological in nature.

radical (RAH-di-kul)
An idea that is radical involves a huge change. Reverend Samuel Barnett and his wife, Henrietta, decided on a radical new approach to help poverty-stricken people.

settlement house (SEH-tul-ment HOWS)
A settlement house is a place in a poor, crowded neighborhood where people can go to get advice, take classes, and more. Jane Addams decided to open a settlement house in Chicago.

stillborn (STIL-born)
A baby that is stillborn is dead at birth. The Addams' ninth child was stillborn.

valedictorian (VAH-luh-dik-TOR-ee-uhn)
A valedictorian is the student who has the highest grades and gives the farewell speech at graduation. Jane Addams was the class valedictorian when she graduated from Rockford Seminary in 1881.

For Further INFORMATION

Web Sites

Visit our homepage for lots of links about Jane Addams:
http://www.childsworld.com/links.html

Note to Parents, Teachers, and Librarians:
We routinely verify our Web links to make sure they're safe,
active sites—so encourage your readers to check them out!

Books

Edge, Laura Bufano. *A Personal Tour of Hull-House.* Minneapolis: Lerner Publications, 2001.

Harvey, Bonnie Carman. *Jane Addams: Nobel Prize Winner and Founder of Hull House.* Berkeley Heights, N.J.: Enslow Publishers, 1999.

Parks, Deborah A. *Jane Addams: Freedom's Innovator.* Alexandria, Va.: Time Life Education, 1999.

Simon, Charnan. *Jane Addams: Pioneer Social Worker.* New York: Children's Press, 1997.

Places to Visit or Contact

Jane Addams Hull-House Museum
To see the original Hull-House building and learn more about the life and work of Jane Addams
University of Illinois at Chicago
800 S. Halsted
Chicago, IL 60607
312/413-5353

Hull-House Association of Chicago
To write for information about the programs sponsored by the organization that still carries on the work of its founder, Jane Addams
10 S. Riverside Plaza, Suite 1700
Chicago, IL 60606
312/906-8600

31

Index

About the Author

PAM ROSENBERG IS A FORMER JUNIOR HIGH SCHOOL TEACHER AND corporate trainer. She currently works as an author and editor of children's books. She has always loved reading and feels very fortunate to be doing work that requires her to read all the time. When she isn't writing or editing books she enjoys spending time with her husband and two children, reading just for fun, and singing with her choir. She lives in Chicago.